Family Photos

On Sunday, we looked at our photos.

"Look at my silly smile!" said Mom. "I don't like this one."

4

"Look at my red face!"
said Dad.
"I don't like this one."

5

"Look at my awful hair!"
said my brother.
"I don't like this one."

"Look at my missing teeth!"
I said.
"I don't like this one."

"Let's throw out the photos we don't like," said Mom.

8

The baby began to cry.

"I don't think the baby wants us to throw out our photos," I said.

CLICK!
"That will be a good photo,"
said Dad.

I showed the photos
to the baby.
The baby began to laugh.